CALUMET CITY PUBLIC LIBRARY

3 1613 00508 5272

W9-AZM-443

J
79611
HOR

STEP BY STEP PROJECTS

How to Make a KITE

CALUMET CITY PUBLIC LIBRARY

Colleen Hord

rourkeeducationalmedia.com

*Scan for Related Titles
and Teacher Resources*

Teaching Focus:

Concepts of Print- Have students find capital letters and punctuation in a sentence. Ask students to explain the purpose for using them in a sentence.

Before Reading:

Building Academic Vocabulary and Background Knowledge

Before reading a book, it is important to set the stage for your child or student by using pre-reading strategies. This will help them develop their vocabulary, increase their reading comprehension, and make connections across the curriculum.

1. Read the title and look at the cover. *Let's make predictions about what this book will be about.*
2. Take a picture walk by talking about the pictures/photographs in the book. Implant the vocabulary as you take the picture walk. Be sure to talk about the text features such as headings, Table of Contents, glossary, bolded words, captions, charts/diagrams, and Index.
3. Have students read the first page of text with you then have students read the remaining text.
4. Strategy Talk – use to assist students while reading.
    - Get your mouth ready
    - Look at the picture
    - Think…does it make sense
    - Think…does it look right
    - Think…does it sound right
    - Chunk it – by looking for a part you know
5. Read it again.
6. After reading the book complete the activities below.

Content Area Vocabulary

breeze
experiments
hobby
inventors
skewers
traffic

After Reading:

Comprehension and Extension Activity

After reading the book, work on the following questions with your child or students in order to check their level of reading comprehension and content mastery.

1. *What does a kite tail do?* (Asking questions)
2. *Explain why it is important to follow directions and attach the skewers before adding the string.* (Infer)
3. *Have you ever flown a kite? Share that experience with us.* (Text to self connection)
4. *Why do you lay the sticks in a cross shape on the plastic bag?* (Asking questions)

Extension Activity

Flying kites can be fun! It is important to remember kite safety when flying. Create a poster illustrating at least one kite safety rule. Share the poster with your family, classmates, or teacher.

Table of Contents

Flying High

Kites are fun to fly, but they can also be useful tools.

Scientists and **inventors** used kites for weather **experiments**, building airplanes, and even for the discovery of electricity!

In June 1752, Benjamin Franklin attempted to prove that lightning is electrical by flying a kite in stormy weather.

Gathering Supplies

You can make your own kite with a few supplies.

You will need:

Plastic shopping bag

Two bamboo **skewers**

Clear tape

Cardboard

Lightweight string

Ruler

Marker

Scissors

Building Your Kite

First, cut open the plastic bag and lay it flat.

Next, snip off the sharp ends of the skewers.

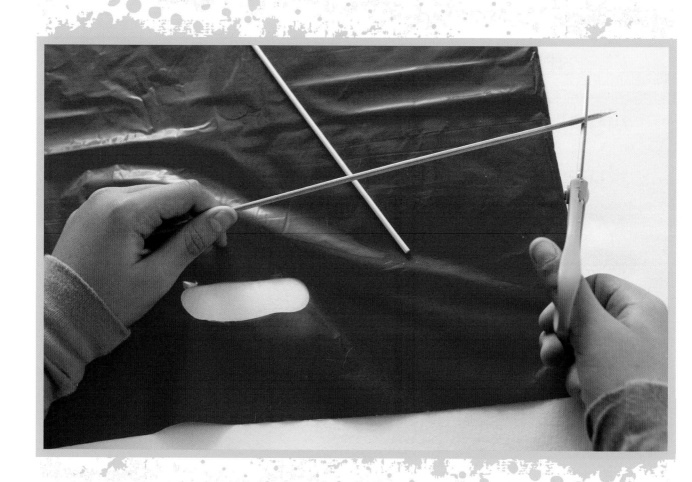

Measure four inches (10 centimeters) down from the top of one stick and make a mark.

Lay the sticks in a cross shape in the middle of the plastic. Place one stick across the four inch (10 centimeter) mark. Mark a dot on the plastic at the end of each stick.

Remove the sticks. Use the marker to
connect the dots. Then, cut out the diamond.

Return your crossed sticks to the plastic.
Use the mark for correct placement. Then
tape the sticks to the plastic.

Roll 50 feet (15 meters) of string around a piece of cardboard for your flying string.

CALUMET CITY PUBLIC LIBRARY

Poke a hole in the plastic where the skewers cross. Then pull the string through. Tie the skewers together with a tight knot.

Cut strips from the leftover plastic for a kite tail. Tape the pieces to the bottom of the kite.

Flying Your Kite

Outside, slowly start running as you unroll the string off your cardboard. Your kite will fly best with a slight **breeze**.

UP, UP, AND AWAY!

Safety First

Be safe when flying your kite. Fly your kite in wide, open spaces away from **traffic** and trees.

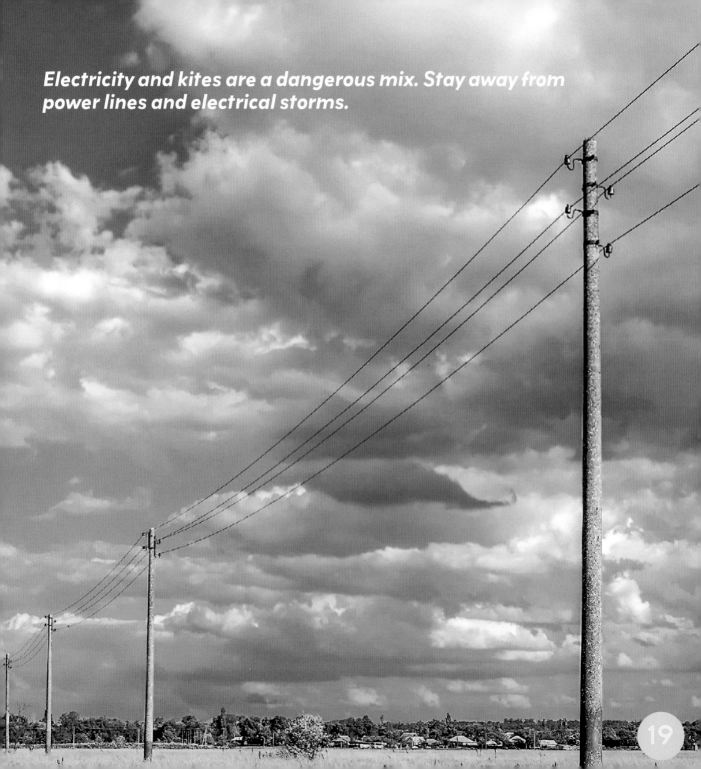

Electricity and kites are a dangerous mix. Stay away from power lines and electrical storms.

Kite flying can be a fun **hobby** for people of all ages.

Photo Glossary

breeze (BREEZ): A gentle wind.

experiments (ek-SPER-uh-ments): Science projects that answer a question.

hobby (HOB-ee): Something that you enjoy doing in your spare time.

inventors (in-VEN-terz): People who think up new things to make.

skewers (SKYOO-urz): Smooth sticks for holding food together while it cooks.

traffic (TRAF-ik): Moving vehicles on a road at a particular time.

Index

Websites to Visit

www.kite.org
www.kitehistory.com
www.grc.nasa.gov/WWW/k-12/airplane/
   kite1.html

Meet The Author!
www.meetREMauthors.com

About the Author

Colleen Hord is an elementary teacher. Her favorite part of her teaching day is Writer's Workshop. She enjoys kayaking, walking on the beach, and watching the birds that nest on her five acres.

© 2016 Rourke Educational Media

All rights reserved. No part of this book may be reproduced or utilized in any form or by any means, electronic or mechanical including photocopying, recording, or by any information storage and retrieval system without permission in writing from the publisher.

www.rourkeeducationalmedia.com

PHOTO CREDITS: All photography by Lisa Marshall Photography except page 4 © yongyut rukkachatsuwa/shutterstock; page 5 courtesy of Library of Congress; page 17 © Lane V. Erickson, page 19 © HaiGala/shutterstock; page 20-21 kan_khampanya/shutterstock; page 22 top © Marcella Raust/shutterstock, middle © e2dan/shutterstock, bottom © CroMary/shutterstock; page 23 top © Photohota/shutterstock, bottom © muh23/shutterstock

Edited by: Keli Sipperley
Cover design and Interior design by: Nicola Stratford
www.nicolastratford.com

Library of Congress PCN Data

How to Make a Kite/ Colleen Hord
(Step-By-Step Projects)
ISBN 978-1-63430-355-2 (hard cover)
ISBN 978-1-63430-455-9 (soft cover)
ISBN 978-1-63430-553-2 (e-Book)
Library of Congress Control Number: 2014934357

Rourke Educational Media
Printed in the United States of America, North Mankato, Minnesota

Also Available as:

ROURKE'S
e-Books